TREME

mc

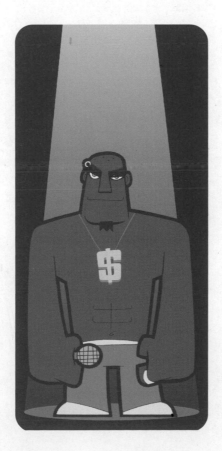

ACKNOWLEDGEMENTS

Big thanks to Tom the editor for all his hard work in making sure you got this book. Big up all the MCs who advised during the writing of this book: you guys rule. And finally, a special hug to the beautiful Annette for her massive support: I love you and everything you do, you make the sunshine, even when the sky ain't blue, that's why our love grew and grew, 'cause you know babe its all true. Peace. Me out.

Printed in the United Kingdom by
MPG Books Ltd, Bodmin

Published by SMT, an imprint of
Sanctuary Publishing Limited
Sanctuary House
45–53 Sinclair Road
London W14 0NS
United Kingdom

www.sanctuarypublishing.com

Copyright: David Sloly, 2004

Picture Credits: Rex Features,
Paul Hampartsoumian, Ed Peto
Design and Editorial: Essential Works

ISBN: 1-84492-036-4

XTREME

mc

David Sloly

smt

CONTENTS

MEET YOUR TUTOR

MC Bling-Bling started rapping when he was a baby. He carried around a plastic microphone (made by Fisher-Price) and repeated 'I can walk and I can talk'. By the time he was ten years old, he had inherited his older brother's ghettoblaster and most of his CD collection. It wasn't long before he figured out that his raps could fit neatly over any tune that didn't already have its own rap. Bling-Bling practised his rhymes and raps in every spare moment and, by the time he turned 16, he was one of the best MCs in the country. Today, he performs throughout the UK, Europe and all over the globe. He's a world-class MC with a lot to say, and a cool and stylish way to say it!

BLING-BLING IS HERE TO...

GUIDE YOU...
Bling-Bling will tell you what you need to know, and show you what to do and how to do it in ten short, easy lessons. Of course, there's some theory to read and learn – but not too much – and plenty of top tips on how to write cool rhymes and how to perform them brilliantly.

TEST YOU...
Each lesson ends with a short test (just so you can see if you're keeping up). But don't be worried – Bling-Bling knows that tests can be a drag so he's made them very bearable.

ADVISE YOU...
Every lesson has advice and tips to help you get on in your writing and rapping. You'll find that Bling-Bling has an easy-to-understand style that can be understood in 'bite-size chunks'. By the end, you'll be amazed at how much you've learned.

MAKE YOU LAUGH...
Writing rhymes has to be fun – if you don't enjoy what you're doing, you'll never get anywhere with it. Writing rhymes is about exposing your soul to the world and letting it all show. Bling-Bling knows that you gotta love doing it – and have a laugh – or it'll look and sound all wrong. So don't worry: Bling-Bling's style will help you relax and let you see the funny side of life.

GENERAL POINTS
In order to learn to MC, you're going to need to buy some gear. Just like any musical instrument, you've got to have one to practise on. If you've already got an MC set-up then fine – you'll learn how to use it. If you haven't got anything yet then wait until you've read a couple of lessons before you buy anything – you'll avoid wasting money on the wrong tools, and probably save a bit of money, too.

But enough of my yakin', let's get RAPPIN'!

THE TOOLS

PENCIL AND PAPER These should become your everyday companions, to stop you from forgetting those amazing thoughts and rhymes that hit you while you're riding on the bus or wa'eva.

MICROPHONE The mic is the main 'axe' that the MC uses to be heard over the music. There are different kinds and different brands, but they all do the same thing – they amplify your voice.

YOUR VOICE This is the most important tool, allowing you to tell the world what you think about everything. It doesn't matter if your voice is high and squeaky, deep and scary or something in-between. MCs' voices come in all shapes and sizes, and there's room for everyone!

MUSIC SYSTEM Nowadays, most DJ's have two record decks or CD players, so that the music never stops…! And the audience never stops dancing! The MC makes the DJ's songs sound personal and alive, and they make it feel special. They make it LIVE. You need music to give you a beat, and to provide a pace and a rhythm for your rhyme and reason. As they say, 'without music, there's no life'.

SO, ARE YOU READY TO BE AN MC?

Find a notebook (the sleeve of this book will do) and a pen or pencil.
These are your tools: like a builder uses a hammer to knock in a nail, the
MC uses pen and paper to take notes of words that sit together and
become his art. The MC finds words that rhyme and bolts them
together and fits them in time.

Sounds hard? Try this:

Look around you! As an MC you'll learn to take inspiration from the
things in life that you see, good and bad. You'll write down on paper all
the things you see and keep them safe (and private so others don't see
your ideas!).

Now look out of the window, what do you see? NOTHING? Look again.
A road with cars, and a house across the street with a garden all neat,
all lit up at night by a yellow streetlight. Look at everything – write, rap
and MC about the real things you see. Practise taking notes about even
the dullest things you notice and make them rhyme. Soon you will be
able to rhyme in real time, drop your lyric real fine. Get the flow on the
go – you're going to start MCing RIGHT NOW.

Let's kick it off with a simple four-line rhyme:

This book contains the lines
That will teach me – the MC – to rhyme
But I won't just drop other people's rhymes
I'll bust my own lyrics and that'll be fine

You see what is happening there? The last word of the first sentence
rhymes with the last word of the second sentence and so on. Now you
try – find some words that rhyme with car:

1. _____
2. _____
3. _____
4. _____
5. _____

(What about 'radar'? And 'sitar'? And 'Go Far'?)

Don't worry too much just yet. Later in the book you're going to learn to
grab words right out of thin air, from here and there, from everywhere;
from low down on the ground and at the top of the stairs.

As an MC you'll be writing words, or as they're called in the business
'lyrics'. By the time you've finished this book, you'll be bustin' lyrics all
over. You'll be writing your own songs. You'll be an MC.

LESSONS

MICROPHONES

The microphone is the most important tool for the MC so you need to know a lot about it. There has never been a pop singer or rapper who hasn't held a microphone in their hand. From Madonna to Justin to Eminem, they all use 'em. Sometimes they use a stand to hold the microphone so they can move their arms around while they perform, and sometimes they have a headset with a built-in microphone so they can dance around the stage. Sometimes they don't appear to have a microphone at all: that's because they're miming and don't need to actually sing or rap. But when they do hold a microphone and sing, they hold it quite close to their mouth – that's so it can pick up their voice clearly. If they held the microphone too far away we wouldn't hear them or it would sound unclear.

YOUR GOALS

GOAL 1
To understand how microphones work.

GOAL 2
To know what kind of microphones are suitable for an MC.

THEORY

A microphone turns your voice into an electrical signal. But don't panic – this electrical signal is a very small current so you won't get an electric shock from it. Once the microphone has turned your voice into an electrical signal, it feeds that signal along the cable attached to the bottom into an amplifier. One end of the microphone usually has a bubble shape to it – that's the end you speak or sing into. In the music industry a microphone is referred to as a 'mic'.

A microphone that you hold in your hand is called a stick microphone. It is made up of three main components: a small disk or plate inside the top section (the pickup), the body (the part you hold), and the socket for the cable that connects the microphone to an amplifier. Some microphones don't need a cable. In a 'radio mic', a tiny radio transmitter sends the audio from the microphone to a receiver that is placed nearby. They're usually bigger than a standard microphone, they have a small aerial at the bottom and they require batteries to work.

If you haven't bought a mic yet, don't worry. To learn to be an MC you don't need one, you can get used to it by using something similar in size or by simply rolling up a piece of card. Bring it on!

There are two basic kinds of microphone:

1. Directional This type of microphone picks up sound from only ONE direction. You have to point the microphone at the source of the sound (your mouth) for it to pick it up. The benefits are that it will eliminate stray sounds (like the crowd or background music) that you don't want.

2. Omni-directional This type of microphone will pick up sounds from all directions, so it's not as good for MCs.

PROBLEM?

If you have an expensive microphone that doesn't work or sounds very faint, it might be because it's a 'powered microphone', which has a tiny pre-amplifier built in to help boost the power. They usually require a battery to operate, and this can be a problem, because if the battery runs low so will the level!

IN PRACTICE

STEP 1

If you SHOUT into your microphone the sound will distort – that's because the pickup is being forced to vibrate too much. If you speak softly with the microphone a long way from your mouth the sound will be very faint. That's because the pickup inside the microphone (which reads the vibration) isn't getting enough sound. The amount of sound is called the 'level'.

STEP 2

You can actually use a pair of headphones as a microphone! Instead of plugging the headphones into the normal headphone socket, plug it into the microphone socket and try speaking into the part that is normally placed next to your ear.

EXERCISE

1. Hold the palm of your hand about one inch from your mouth and say the word 'PLEASE'. Did you feel the rush of air as you said the word?

2. Now hold your hand about twice that distance from your mouth and repeat the word. Feel that the rush of air is lighter, softer.

3. Now go to a window, place your fingertips on the glass and, with the other hand, lightly tap on the window. Can you feel the vibration passing through the glass and onto your fingertips?

A microphone works by detecting sounds, and sounds are made up of vibrations. Vibrations travel through the air just the same way as they do through the glass. The microphone can pick up the tiniest of vibrations and convert them into an electrical signal. Inside the microphone is a very thin disc. This disc is what reads the vibration. The thin disc is often called the 'pickup'.

TEST

QUESTION 1
What are the two basic kinds of microphone?

QUESTION 2
What is a radio mic?

QUESTION 3
What causes mic distortion?

MIC TECHNIQUE

Once you own a microphone, it's crucially important to take good care of it. As an MC you will rely on your microphone to make your voice sound clear. But it's also important to use good 'mic technique' to get a good sound. Speaking or singing into a mic isn't as easy as it might seem. You need to know how to control the volume and how to avoid the common problems that can so easily ruin your sound.

YOUR GOALS

GOAL 1
To know what to look for when choosing a mic.

GOAL 2
To develop your 'mic technique'.

THEORY

We've seen how important a good microphone is to you as an MC, so be careful when buying a new or used mic. Some microphones may look brilliant but are too heavy to hold in a performance, and some mics seem attractive because they're so cheap, but beware they are probably rubbish! Be sure to TRY BEFORE YOU BUY. Any good shop will let you try out a microphone first. Try at least three so you can hear the difference. Repeat the same rhyme in each microphone to compare how they sound – and, ideally, bring a friend with you to help decide which one sounds the best.

There are four important rules about microphones:

1. Always grip the mic firmly so that you don't drop it.

2. If you're wearing rings, be aware that if they tap against the body of the mic the sound will be picked up and amplified (though this could be something you could incorporate into your style!) Try tapping out your own rhythm over the top of the tune – but be warned: if your tapping isn't in time, it will ruin your rhyme.

3. The lead that connects to the bottom of the mic can also transfer sound to the pickup (that's vibration for you). So be sure that it is not tapping against anything, like the floor or a table.

4. Try to spit as little as possible into the mic – they usually come with a soft shield to help stop moisture build-up – but some spit will always get in there. If the moisture builds up on the pickup inside the mic, it will not read the vibrations of sound properly and before long it will sound distorted. Always keep the cover on but, if it does get wet, try hanging it upside down for a few minutes.

TIP

Used microphones are the cheapest option, and good deals are out there to be had. Microphones with a metal body are generally well built and will last a long time if they have been cared for. They are fairly simple and not much can go wrong with them. If the sound is clear and good then the mic probably hasn't been abused too much.

IN PRACTICE

STEP 1

How should you hold your mic? Experiment by holding it in different ways until you feel comfortable with it. Practise your rhymes holding it one way and then another to see how it affects your ability to speak comfortably. Have a look at yourself holding the mic in the mirror to see what looks cool for you. How close should you hold your microphone to your mouth? Again, it depends on how loud you MC. Some MCs push the mic right into their lips but, when they shout, the audience can't hear anything they are saying! The right distance depends on how you rap.

STEP 2

'Popping' describes the sound made when a rush of air goes into a microphone and causes it to make a deep booming or popping sound. Words that start with a 'P' are the most likely to cause this to happen. To avoid popping: hold your mic to your mouth, MC as normal and, just before you get to a word that starts with a P, turn your head slightly to the left or right so that the word is not spoken directly into the microphone.

PROBLEM?

The usual problem with microphones is dodgy connections in the cable. Cables and mics usually have soldered plugs, sometimes at both ends. These solder joints can become loose and cause the sound to cut in and out (so no yanking on the cable!). Always keep a spare cable handy and change when necessary.

EXERCISE

1. Experiment with the mic by holding it at different angles and distances from your lips until the sound is good and the level is right (not too loud and not too faint).

TEST

QUESTION 1
What is 'popping'?

QUESTION 2
How can popping be avoided?

QUESTION 3
How far from the mouth should a mic be held?

CONNECTING UP

Now let's look at how to connect up the MC's gear to different kinds of equipment, like a home hi-fi or a computer. Whatever system you use, the basic layout and fundamentals are the same.

YOUR GOALS

GOAL 1
To connect the mic to a hi-fi.

GOAL 2
To connect the mic to a computer.

GOAL 3
To connect the mic to a DJ console or mixer.

THEORY

Every piece of equipment you come across as an MC will be slightly different in look and operation. Once you've got used to the different cables, plugs and sockets it gets easier for you to connect your microphone and get MCing.

TIP

Some consoles have a 'dip' mode designed to turn the volume of the music DOWN when speaking through the mic... Be sure to turn that one off as its not meant for MCing.

IN PRACTICE

CONNECTING YOUR MICROPHONE TO A HI-FI

Let's start by looking at a hi-fi. The home hi-fi can usually play CDs and tapes and maybe even records. On the front it will have all the usual buttons, but it might also have a socket to plug in a microphone. If so, you can start rapping the moment you get your hands on a microphone by just plugging it in here. (If your hi-fi has a 'karaoke' feature, you'll easily be able to MC over CDs and maybe even over the radio!) If not, you'll probably need to buy an adaptor or, more probably, a small microphone 'pre-amp' so that you can plug your mic into the 'auxiliary' input on the back of the system (check your manual to be sure of this).

STEP 1

Once you've got the mic plugged in, turn up the volume (gently at first) and check that the sound is coming out of the speakers. For now, try speaking a few words into the mic and, if possible, try to record them on a tape to see if it's all working. If the tape works quickly and easily for you, then experiment holding the microphone at different distances from your mouth until your recording is as clear as possible on playback.

Some equipment will have a 'microphone level' which often looks like two bars of lights or needles that swing from left to right with the volume. If the meter reads red then your level is too high and the sound may distort (ie sound rubbish). Try to keep the levels in the green but still high enough (with enough power) to get your voice out there.

PROBLEM?

If, when you plug in the mic and turn it up, you get a whiney howling sound (feedback) then you'll need to (quickly) move the microphone AWAY from the speakers or turn the speakers in the opposite direction.

STEP 2

(CONNECTING YOUR MICROPHONE TO A COMPUTER)

Computers tend to have tiny 'mini-jack' sockets (a ⅛ inch-wide hole) at the back. Most often, there will be three sockets of this size: one for headphones, one for external speakers and one for a microphone (you'll know by the little picture of a mic next to the correct hole). The internal sound card of the computer will determine how good the sound quality is (and you can't control this without a lot of money and hassle) but, for now, plug in your microphone and select (or download) a program that enables you to record your voice and play it back.

There are plenty of programs you can download from the Internet, such as:

1. www.vanbasco.com Aimed at the karaoke market but will give you an idea of software that is designed to sing along to.

2. www.koolkaraokestudio.com Lets you buy music without lyrics so you can rap along. They have a few tracks to MC over.

3. www.pcdj.com Has some hip hop production software that will get you recording your rhymes and mixing it with music.

STEP 3

(CONNECTING YOUR MICROPHONE TO A DJ CONSOLE)

If you've got a DJ set-up, the connections are even easier. The mixer will almost certainly have a ¼ inch jack socket that is marked 'mic', though it could be on the front, on the top or even on the back panel. Find the controls that adjust the volume of the microphone (usually marked 'mic') before you plug it in (otherwise you may get feedback!).

EXERCISE

1. Once you've plugged it in, gently turn up the mic volume until you can hear your voice. Put on a record and have a go at speaking over the music.

2. Adjust the levels until you can hear the music clearly and the sound of your voice clearly too.

TEST

QUESTION 1
What three kinds of set-ups can a microphone be plugged into?

QUESTION 2
What is a 'dip' mode on a DJ mixer?

QUESTION 3
What's the quickest way to stop feedback?

MCING WITH A DJ

It's very common for an MC to join forces with a DJ to perform. While the DJ plays the music, the MC drops lyrics on the mic. The combined effort of both DJ and MC makes an action-packed performance that's far better than either could do alone.

Professional MCs have to work with different DJs all the time, so they need to be able to adapt to different DJ styles. It can be quite nerve-racking the first time an MC performs with a DJ. The MC has to watch and listen to understand what the DJ is playing and to hear how he is blending the different tunes together. The MC needs to remember his rhymes and perform with passion and care, while listening to what the DJ is doing and reacting to the DJ's set. It ain't easy, man…!

YOUR GOALS

GOAL 1
To understand what a DJ does so that you can work with him/her (not against him/her).

GOAL 2
To adjust your sound and to use effects to your advantage.

THEORY

In the most basic terms, the DJ's job is to keep the people on the dancefloor dancing. He does this by selecting and playing music that the audience will like and by creating a seamless flow of music that never drops a beat. The MC has to know when to drop his rhymes – and when to shut up.

IN PRACTICE

STEP 1

It's important to choose a good place to stand during your MC performance. You must be facing the audience but you don't want to be standing in front of the DJ. Make sure the mic lead is long enough and has plenty of slack so you can move around. Most importantly, don't stand in front of the speakers as this will cause feedback. Finally, adjust the microphone volume to the correct level to find an equal balance between your voice and the music. The audience should be able to hear the music clearly while also hearing and understanding your rap.

STEP 2

Some mixer consoles offer a few controls, called 'EQ' (tone control), to adjust the way the voice will sound. The EQ allows a manual adjustment of the amount of bass, middle and treble in your voice.

You'll need to experiment with these to best suit your own voice, but the basics are that the BASS will adjust the lower end of your vocal range (to make the voice boom more, but not necessarily make your voice sound any deeper). The MID or MIDDLE will adjust the middle of your vocal range (and if turned up full with the bass turned down, you'll sound like you're on a telephone call – maybe that is an effect you can use in your MC set!). The TREBLE will adjust the top end of your vocal range, and, if turned up, will add clarity to your voice and make the words easier to understand.

Experiment with EQ as much as possible to find the best sound for your own voice. Be careful, however, because EQ can create effects on your voice that are quite disturbing and may even damage your speakers if too extreme.

STEP 3

EFFECTS

Some DJ mixers (and most computer MC and DJ programs) have built-in effects that can be quickly and easily turned on.

These effects usually include:

ECHO To make your lyrics repeat (over, over, over, over...).

REVERB To create the impression that you're in a big room or concert hall.

DISTORTION To make your voice sound distorted (yes! It can be really cool!).

FLANGER To create a metallic or robotic quality.

If your equipment offers any of these, experiment to find one that you like, then write it down so you can find it again when you want to use it. If not, don't worry – if your rhymes are smokin', you don't really need anything else.

STEP 4

THE MC AND THE DJ

Now you're all connected up and you know what buttons do what. The DJ is spinning tunes and you're ready to drop rhymes. Spit your lyrics into the crowd and watch them go crazy. Get the name of the DJ in your head before you start to rap. Work with the DJ now – listen carefully to the music and bounce along to it. Bouncing to the music will help you keep in time and sound sharp. If the music has lyrics of its own then be careful not to rhyme over the lyrics of the song, because it will spoil the song. Wait for breaks in the tune and then drop a rhythm.

PROBLEM?

If your EQ effects cause feedback in the system, try using less TREBLE EQ or even turn the TREBLE down a bit, as this usually makes the hi-pitched whine stop.

EXERCISE

1. Try plugging your mic into a DJ mixer (your own if you have one, or a mate's if you can borrow it or use it within his or her set-up).

2. Try turning the various EQ buttons and knobs up and down to hear what effect each one has.

3. Try adding effects such as reverb and echo, and note which settings you think make your voice sound better.

TIP

Make eye contact with the DJ as often as possible to gauge him – is he loving it? The easiest way to get the DJ on-side is to big them up: 'Put your hands in the air if the DJ is mashing up the tunes big time – show your respect and let me hear you scream if you love this tune.' If you and the DJ look like you're having the time of your life, then the crowd will enjoy it too.

TEST

QUESTION 1
What does a DJ do?

QUESTION 2
What is an EQ?

QUESTION 3
Name three different effects that can be used on a voice?

WRITING RHYMES

Rhymes can come into your mind at any time, so you should be carrying a pen and paper with you at all times by now. In order to MC properly, you always need goods rhymes – lyrics, words, something to say – and you need lots of 'em. To start with, you could just copy other MCs' lyrics – but to be in a class of your own, you will need to find your own 'voice'.

YOUR GOALS

GOAL 1
To understand the writing process.

GOAL 2
To write original material.

GOAL 3
To find inspiration.

THEORY

Writing rhymes is all about telling stories: you have something to say and you say it in your own way. And to tell a good story – in order to really grab an audience – there must be a beginning, middle and end. The beginning explains what the story is about, it sets the scene and it gives the story a start. The middle is the main body of the story, with people, events and facts. It explains 'who, what, why, when, where and how'; it carries the story along to the end (or what is sometimes called the 'close'). The close completes the story and gives the 'pay off' (the resolution or climax).

IN PRACTICE

There's only one way to begin and that's to begin. Just put pen to paper and see what comes out. So what will be your first rap? Your first lyrical smack? Start with a subject that you already know. Take something that you do every day, and find the words to describe that subject in some shape, way or fashion and with those words we'll begin to play.

STEP 1

Making the bed. Silly subject I know, but it's the first thing I have to do in the morning and I hate it; I just want to eat some cereal and watch TV. But what possible rhyme can we come up with to MC about making a bed in the morning? First of all, let's look at all the words that are connected to this chore...

Bed
Covers
Sheets

Now, add some more of your own words to the list. Write down any sentences that describe making a bed. Like...

Throwing covers in the air
Tucking in sheets
Waking in the morning

STEP 2

Now, let's start building a rhyme using what we have so far and adding in some extra lyrics.

I wake up in the morning	**(the beginning)**
Know the first thing I must do	**(middle)**
Is a job that is boring	**(middle)**
But only takes a minute or two	**(middle)**
I throw the covers in the air	**(middle)**
Some go here, some go there	**(more middle)**
Tucking in the sheets	**(more middle)**
When I should be making beats	**(even more middle)**
But when I have the job done	**(starting to close)**
I can leave the bedroom	**(about to close)**
And have some first-class fun	**(close and end)**

STEP 3

Alright, you wouldn't go on stage in front of a bunch of people and chant that little number I admit, but let's look at how I wrote it.

First, I took a subject matter – in this case, making the bed. Then, I noted some words that are related to the subject. And finally, I put them together into a little rhyme. The subject wasn't important. What was important was the relationship between the words and the story those words told.

So how do you come up with words that rhyme together? The answer is simple – use the alphabet. Take the word that you want to use. Let's say, for example, the word is 'grey'. Now starting with the first letter of the alphabet, A, swap the 'g' of grey for each new letter of the alphabet to make new words. And don't worry if those new words are longer or shorter than the first one. Some examples are array, betray, clay, day, fray, hay – and you should do that all the way through the alphabet. That's why it's so important to have a notebook – to write all these test words down until you find the ones that work in your story.

STEP 4

> (BE YOURSELF!)

To be a true MC
That can become a star
You be a real MC
By being who you are

> (CHOOSE A STYLE)

Any style of your choice
But always use
Your real true voice

> (DRESS UP IN CLOTHES)

That makes you feel good
But if you're from the suburbs
Then don't pretend you're from the hood

PROBLEM?

Some rhymes are hard to drop, they leave you tongue-tied and make the lyric a flop. So to overcome this potential nightmare, just look in a mirror and stare. Look at the reflection of your mouth as you say your lines – keep watching, keep repeating and soon it'll all be fine.

STEP 5

Don't worry if you have trouble spelling difficult words – it's OK to make mistakes. But try to keep a dictionary close by, because, after all, you are an MC now and it's important that you become the master of your trade. Check words that you have trouble spelling AFTER you have got your rhyme down on paper. Some dictionaries will even show you how words should be pronounced and this is helpful when learning new or difficult words that may be unusual (but work well in your song). Practise saying the words facing a mirror and exaggerate the movement of your lips as you repeat the word over and over.

STEP 6

Handwriting is important (as you'll need to be able to go back and read your lyrics at a later date), so be neat and clear. It sometimes helps to write certain words bigger or in capitals to remember that they're important or that they should be stressed. (And try using all capital letters if you find you're having difficulties reading back your lyrics.)

STEP 7

'Writer's block' is when you just can't think of anything to write – and it's a well-known problem for anyone creating art using words. When it strikes, you'll suddenly feel empty, void of all inspiration and unable to come up with anything worth writing down. When this happens to me, I just go back to my notebooks and look at old stuff written in the past. Sometimes I can find a new inspiration in a half-finished rhyme to get me going again. That's why it's important to always have your notebook with you; when it's full put it away in a drawer so you can go back to it whenever.

Another way to get around writer's block and feel inspired is to keep a list of subjects that you may want to write about. If I'm on a trip, say, on a train, I'll write notes like: 'TRAVEL, super-fast train rocking side to side as it glides through the countryside. I ride to the beach to seek out the high tide, swim with the sharks and the chloride.' I can go back to these thoughts when I have some spare time and work them up into a rhyme.

Quite often inspiration can come from an emotion, like when you feel excited about something or frightened, sad or angry. These are good times to make notes; you can make all the words rhyme later, but first just get the raw thoughts and emotions down on paper.

TIP

A computer is great for saving lyrics, e-mailing them to friends, editing, organising and printing. But most computers are not very portable, (even laptop computers are always a bit of a struggle) and they're too fragile. For day-to-day use, go for the good old pen and paper – it's cheap, easy to use on a bus, never crashes and the batteries never run out!

EXERCISE

1. When you practise, try to hear the beats in your head and repeat the same rhyme you just said.

2. Jump around, as you rhyme to the beat, keep the flow natural and sweet.

3. Move your body and shuffle your feet. Lyrical content is what you eat, drink and sleep.

TEST

QUESTION 1
What's a good way to find a rhyme when you're stuck?

QUESTION 2
What is 'writer's block'?

QUESTION 3
What are some useful books for writing rhymes?

DELIVERY

Who are you? Being yourself in front of a microphone can seem very hard at first. It takes time, patience and practise to become comfortable with your natural MC voice. Some MCs are cool with the way their voice sounds straight away and feel comfortable with what they hear. Others love the sound of their own voice too much and are sometimes guilty of going too far when they get the chance to hold a microphone.

Most of us, however, cringe at the first recorded playback we hear of ourselves dropping rhymes or even just speaking. It never sounds like we imagine it to sound when we are talking to friends. It may sound high-pitched or weak. This is because our ear, or more precisely our 'hearing', compensates for background noise, visual perceptions, slight variants in volume and other distractions. But the microphone cannot and does not do this – it just accurately replicates what it processes. What you say is what you get.

YOUR GOALS

GOAL 1
To choose an MC name.

GOAL 2
To find your own 'voice'.

GOAL 3
To improve your voice through exercise.

THEORY

There are no rules
To selecting a name
Take a name from a book
Or a Playstation game
Use a nickname
Your real name
MC Gold or MC Mike
Choose any name you want
Just choose one you like

An MC's delivery is based on his 'attitude', which comprises the whole package: style, rhymes, speed, confidence, visual look, physical moves and, not least, the MC's name. (So, it's important to get the details right!) Most young MCs will begin by using a delivery 'borrowed' from someone they admire or respect. That's not a problem at first but, after a while, everyone needs to develop, grow and find their own true self.

I'm MC Lucy
From Class 4C
Got lyrics in my pocket
Written by me

I'm MC Paul
Number one in the place
Got the fastest rhymes
And I'm winning the race

I'm Mr MC Bass
Showing my face
Rhymes on time
All over the place

I'm an MC
MC Jiggle It Right
When I get going on the mic
I can go all night

IN PRACTICE

STEP 1

Your MC name can be anything you want it to be. Mr Bounce or Mr Loose, MC Rabbit, MC Bike – whatever you like. Let your imagination run wild when thinking about new names. Try walking around your bedroom and name things out aloud: computer, mouse, monitor (actually, I like 'MC Monitor' – good name!). Ideally, your MC name should be easy to remember and smooth to pronounce. MC 'Rumble In The Jungle With A Monkey On My Shoulder' is probably too long for a name, but you can always change it if you stop liking it.

After practising a few rhymes, ask yourself:

1. Does it sound like I'm trying too hard?
2. Do I sound confident?
3. Do I talk to my closest friends like this?
4. Have I suddenly got a different accent?

STEP 2

If it sounds like you are trying too hard, then you probably are. You may be overdoing it to compensate for not knowing all your lyrics. It could be that you have too many lyrics and should be using fewer words. Make it as simple as possible for yourself in these early stages.

Check me
I'm an MC
My name is MC Yellow Bee

STEP 3

Confidence comes with practise, and a lack of confidence can make the voice sound a little fragile. If your voice sounds lost and weak, try not to shout to compensate, but rather try this: recite your lyrics standing up with your head looking straight ahead and move your whole body side to side as you drop rhythms. If at all possible, do this in front of a large mirror or even standing on your bed. The wobbly mattress, sinking into the bed as you rock from side to side, should force you to concentrate on balance as well as lyrics – and, since most people say that their legs are like jelly on stage, having practised on a wobbly bed in advance, you won't notice much difference!

PROBLEM?

If you have trouble remembering or spitting out your lyrics, practise reciting your rhymes without notes at a faster speed than normal. This will make it seem easier when you later deliver the same rhymes at a slower speed.

Developing a bit of confidence in your delivery will help you settle on a style of delivery – even if your new 'voice' sounds unnatural to you at first. It's not uncommon for an MC to use a different tone or style of voice when performing. (And, if you think about it, you'll notice how you speak differently when you talk to a parent or teacher compared to your friends. So, already you have more than one voice!) You need to find the one you like best for your MCing. But it must be YOUR OWN voice; try to stop yourself from imitating someone else. When in doubt – return to your most comfortable speaking voice.

Another strange phenomenon that afflicts some MCs is a sudden change of accent. If it works for you then great, but be careful of taking on a foreign voice just for the sake of it (ie if you're from Liverpool then you probably shouldn't sound like you're from New York!). Sounding like other people usually means you're copying someone else's style, and you've got to be yourself now, so concentrate on dropping your own lyrics with your own style.

STEP 4

The best way to learn your rhymes is to read them aloud. Practise them at half speed first, so your brain has time to read the words from the page, and put them into your memory, while at the same time instructing your mouth to say them aloud (PHEW!). If the rhyme you are practising is long, break it down into four-line parts, and learn four lines a day. Keep repeating them aloud until you can deliver the whole rhyme without it being written down in front of you.

I got something to say
You need to hear
I got lyrics on my mind
And they're loud and clear

STEP 5

Of course, you have to remember them too so, once you've learned them, keep practising so that you don't forget.

Practise silently in your head.
Practise in front of the mirror instead,
Practise in the bath,
Practise recording your voice
Listening back and having a laugh.

Every day when you get up you should spend a little time reading your MC lyrics. Then you can repeat them back on the way to school, at break and again on the way home. Soon the lyrics will become etched in your mind. When you are performing you will no longer be trying to remember the next word; you will know them all as naturally as you know your own name.

STEP 6

Training your voice is important. Your voice comes from your vocal chords, which are like any other muscle on your body (including your brain), and, if exercised correctly, they will become stronger. Yes! It is possible to train your voice to give it a richer sound! Check out the following exercises and practise properly, regularly and hard.

EXERCISE

OK, write down your MC name (here) ....
If you don't have one then now's the time to think up a name for yourself.

DAILY EXERCISE

1. Make an 'arhh' sound and listen to the constant sound. Try to keep it as one continuous noise and don't let it go up or down in volume or in tone.

2. Relax your throat muscles by tilting your head back slightly. Feel the air coming up from your stomach, from deep inside you, which is needed for the 'arhh' to make its journey up through the chest, passing your relaxed throat and out of a wide-open mouth.

3. Once you can get a constant 'arhh', practise taking a deep breath and releasing it gently (and with measure) as you make the 'arhh' sound.

4. See how long you can keep it going without your voice wavering. Remember you can do this anywhere – such as when you're riding your bike or doing chores around the house!

5. When you've gotten pretty good at this, practise using the same method, but replace the 'arhh' with an 'A'. Say the letter A and hold it steady (AAAAAAAAAAAAA), always breathing out at a constant rate, gently pushing the air from your stomach up through your chest and past a relaxed throat.

6. Once you can hold a good A try the same with E, C and D, each time going up in pitch (higher and higher, but not too high). Each time you practise, try taking it a little deeper in tonality.

REMEMBER, never overwork your vocal chords: five to ten minutes each day is enough!

MUSIC BASICS

Every MC needs to understand the elements and the basics of music. Let's start right at the beginning. All music comes from instruments (including the human voice) played by musicians. Musicians are singers singing, guitarists playing and…MCs dropping lyrical content. (Yes! You are a musician! Don't forget it!)

YOUR GOALS

GOAL 1
To understand how the basic elements of music fit together.

GOAL 2
To understand how the rhythm and beat control the MC's rhyme.

THEORY

You'll come across all kinds of different sounds when you're listening to your music: from drums and pianos to sound effects of cars skidding and freaky alien noises. These are all instruments of music. They all go into building the tune and giving it a style, a sound and an emotion or feeling. MCs need to understand how a collection of instruments (including the voice) work together to make music. If musicians don't follow each other and work together, the music will be rubbish!

Imagine for a moment that you are riding along on a bicycle. The pedals of the bicycle are like the drummer. The faster you pedal, the quicker the beat of the drum: boom, boom, boom, boom. The wheels of the bicycle are like a deep bass sound. The bass sound follows at the same speed as the drum beat. Imagine the handlebars are like a singer. The singer (or the MC), like the handlebars, can send the song in a different direction, but can't change the speed, or the tempo, of the song. All the instruments have to work together at just the right speed.

Hands on the handlebars
Bum on the seat
Feet turning pedals
To the speed of the beat

Your feet are on the pedal
The pedals are going around
When one is all the way up
Make a loud drum sound

When the next one is pointing
Down at the ground
It's time for you to make
That drum sound drum sound

Hands on the handlebars
Bum on the seat
Feet turning pedals
To the speed of the beat

Now I hear the bass
Playing real deep
Keeping in time
To the beat to the beat

Not too fast and not too slow
Guitar, sitar, trombone and piano
Trumpet, electronic bleeps
All of us together to the beat

Now the MC has joined in too
Spitting words the way we do

The keyboards, guitars, bongo drums too
The piano, trumpet and a gentle flute
...hang on – what about the drum?

TIP

When you're trying to feel the mood of the music, listen to the mood of the drummer. A tune with sparse drums probably doesn't want a fast rap, while a tune with banging bass and snares is probably crying out for fast-as-lightning rhymes!

IN PRACTICE

In dance music, the drum is used to count the beats that the musicians keep time to. You can keep time with the drum by counting along with each main drumbeat (1234, 2234, 3234, 4234, 1234, 2234, 3234, 4234, and so on). While tapping your foot in time to the music, lift your arm as if holding a microphone. Now nod your head gently in time with music – now you're following the beat!

Every song has its own beat, though some beats will be faster than others and some will be slower. The speed (or 'tempo') of a song is measured in 'beats per minute' (or bpm), which is simply the number of beats that go by in one minute. A tune keeps a constant speed, or bpm, from start to finish, so your foot-tapping shouldn't speed up or slow down during a song.

A tune that runs at 80 bpm is quite slow, while 145 bpm is very fast. An MC must adapt his speed of delivery to fit in with the bpm of the tune, so a drum'n'bass MC would spit rhymes quicker than an R&B MC in order to keep up with the faster bpm. Different horses for different courses. Different strokes for different folks.

STEP 1

Try this nice and slow:

Drop lyrical content slow on the R&B
Give the audience plenty of time to spot me
Stage lights change colour to a yellow glow
Shows off my gold and my lyrical flow
Hurry up for the drum'n'bass MC
Moves faster than a shark in the sea

PROBLEM?

If you're trying to rap over a tune you've never heard before and you're worried about fitting in, try to rap short words and quick rhythms so that you can easily pull back if you have to suddenly stop.

STEP 2

Now, try this much faster:

Just time for 123
Check my rhymes
They're speedy
Jamming
D 'n' B
123
Time to get cheeky
Here comes the sneaky
Bass line
Rumble is fine
Blowing up my speakers
All of the time

MUSIC FOR MCs: RULES

1. Never MC over the singer. Two voices at the same time will make it impossible for the audience to understand what the singer is singing or the MC is saying.

2. Always follow the speed of the song. The most important instrument in a tune for an MC to focus on is the drum, so as to keep a constant beat. By always tapping your foot along to the drum beat you can be sure you aren't dropping rhymes too fast or too slow.

3. Don't be too shy to show some emotion and feel the mood of the music. Standing very still, looking at the floor for half an hour, isn't going to entice a crowd of people to feel your energy! You need to move your arms, body and legs as well as your mouth. You need to emphasise certain words to bring some drama to the music. Always try to reflect the attitude of the tune in your style of rap – if the tune is hyped-up, get hyped; if the tune is sleepy, then relax.

4. MCs often rap over tunes that also have singing in them, and the best way to avoid clashing with a singer is always to know the tune well. If it's on CD then you can read the CD machine's time counter to learn the song: if the singer starts at 00:44 then you will know that you can drop rhymes up to that point. If the vocals stop at 1:29, then you know when to start dropping rhymes again.

5. If you're MCing with a live DJ, you should aim to drop rhymes when the DJ is mixing two records together. If the tunes the DJ is playing are ones you haven't heard before, then you'll have to listen carefully for natural breaks in the singing, when you can drop short rhymes – but you have to stay alert and be able to stop quickly if the singer starts singing again unexpectedly.

6. If the music is instrumental (no singer) then just spit your rhymes with an even flow. Drop some rhymes then hang back and let the music role drop some more just as the tune is about to blow. Drum'n'bass tunes build up in instruments as the tune plays through: the music builds up and up until it hits a 'breakdown' (that's when the drum stops and the track becomes quiet). Then the instruments will build up and up until the drum kicks back in – this is the best point to drop a new rhyme – just as the tune kicks back in. The crowd will love it: all the instruments pounding along and you rhyming and feeding off the energy of the music.

EXERCISE

1. Choose a song for rapping that has singing as well as instrumental bits. Write down the start and stop times of the singing on the CD and then write and spit out your own lyrics to go in the gaps in-between.

TEST

QUESTION 1
Why does it help to tap your foot along with the music?

QUESTION 2
What measures the speed of a song?

QUESTION 3
What's an 'instrumental'?

PERFORMING LIVE

Live performance lets you show off the rhymes you've written and learned, but it takes courage and skill to perform infront of anybody (2 or 2,000 people!). Even if you find that you don't actually like performing, that doesn't mean you shouldn't enjoy writing lyrics and rapping them for your own fun! Likewise, if you like writing lyrics but don't want to perform, you might try to team up with another MC who can drop your lyrics for you. Or it could be that you love performing but don't have a ready supply of lyrics, in which case a partner might help. Whatever you choose, practise hard and often, try performing in front of a mirror and always give it 100 per cent.

YOUR GOALS

GOAL 1
To understand the key aspects of performing.

GOAL 2
To properly organise your own performance.

THEORY

Performance is all about preparation. Of course the most important thing is practise, but you also have to find an audience, a place to perform (even if it's your front room), do a 'sound check', calm your nerves and finally throw down your rhymes.

Bish bash bosh
Oh my gosh
On stage like Posh
Feeling the rush

I MC day by day
Practise
Everything I say
Sound check
With the lyrics I play
Perform
Live on stage

IN PRACTICE

SOUND CHECKING

STEP 1

Before any performance you always need to check that everything is ready and working: that your microphone is plugged in and working properly.

STEP 2

The three most important things you want to be sure of before performing are:

1. Your voice, and the music, is coming out of the speakers.
2. Your voice is clear enough so that the audience can understand what you're saying.
3. Your voice is not too loud or too quiet in the mix (but 'balanced' nicely with the music).

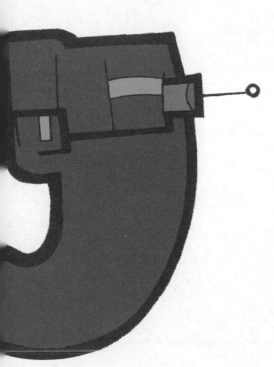

DEALING WITH NERVES

Everyone, including the biggest star on TV, gets nervous before a performance. Feeling nervous before you perform is normal. But you have to try to keep your nerves in check, and not let them get the better of you.

If you start to feel overwhelmed with nerves before a performance (and you will) then try to think only about what you will do once you get on stage:

STEP 1

Practise your rhymes quietly to yourself, saying them clearly and slowly.

STEP 2

Another method to help stay in control is to breathe in slowly and deeply through your nose and then breathe out very slowly through a partially open mouth.

STEP 3

Be ready for (and expect) nervousness BEFORE you even leave your house to go to the gig. Help yourself to stay calm by concentrating on your lyrics, and maybe even use the nerves to inspire some new rhymes. (Use everything that ever happens to you in your lyrics!)

One stage
Rolling with rage
No holding back
I been locked in my cage

For too long
What can go wrong
Nerves got hold of me
Before I come on

Dropping first class rhyme
Star of the prime time
Backing out now
Would be a crime

THE AUDIENCE

Whether it's your friends, your club or your parents, whoever is listening to you perform becomes your audience. And, just like professionals, it's the audience that you're performing to and for. The enjoyment of the audience must always come first.

STEP 1

Before you perform in front of anyone, take a moment to look at them and see what they're already doing. If they're dancing and having a great time to the music, then it'll be pretty easy for you to keep them dancing.

STEP 2

If, however, they're not dancing, then you'll have to work a little harder to win them over. You can do this by including and encouraging the audience in your performance: 'Put your hands together if you're from Fairholm School,' or 'Let's make some noise in the house and get this party started, people.'

> **TIP**
> When you're trying to liven up your performance, rap the word 'joy' and try stretching one arm out to the side or, if you want to use the word 'pain', pull your arms in tight over your stomach. This is called 'embellishing your performance' and without it an MC can be a bit boring.

HAVE SOME RESPECT

PROBLEM?

If you have a particularly bad problem with nerves, try closing your eyes when you practise at home and imagine an enormous crowd in front of you. Speak to the 'crowd' and imagine getting responses from them. The more real you can imagine the 'crowd' to be, the more your practise will set you up for the real thing.

STEP 1

Never make fun of your audience or abuse the power you have as an MC by being rude or dissing people. And that includes your friends who might know that you're only 'having some fun'. For the rest of the audience, it's boring and exclusive.

STEP 2

As an MC, always have respect and try to make everyone in the audience feel included: after all, you'll want everyone to come and see you perform again!

Don't diss me
When I'm gone
You'll miss me
I'm your MC
Crowd friendly
Spitting lyrics
Like 123
Everybody is listening to me
What you think I do this for free
I MC because that's who I be
In crowd respect I have a degree

STEP 1

Once you've written and learned a few rhymes, you can have some fun arranging your own MC parties for friends and family. (Maybe one of your friends is going to have a party and you could do your MCing there – you've got to start somewhere!)

STEP 2

There may be other MCs in your neighbourhood or school. Ask if you could team up with them to perform in turn at a party.

Give me a mic and I'll have a crack
Record me on tape and I'll listen back
If my rhymes are rubbish give me the sack
Or tell me what you think I lack

EXERCISE

1. Try doing your own 'gig' by setting up your music system on some sort of 'stage' in a room with a few chairs and invite some family and friends to come and listen. It ain't Wembley Stadium, but even Eminem had to start somewhere.

TEST

QUESTION 1
What is a 'soundcheck'?

QUESTION 2
What can an MC do to calm his nerves before a gig?

QUESTION 3
What's it all for?

RECORDING

Everyone is always surprised at how different they sound when they listen back to a recording of their own voice, and it can often be a mortifying experience. Try to ignore the feelings of embarrassment and remember that everyone else hears you speak everyday and they never think your voice sounds embarrassing! Listening back to recordings of yourself is a great way to measure how good you have become at keeping time when dropping rhymes. You can analyse your recordings over time to hear how your MCing is coming on.

THEORY

A great way to attract attention to what you're doing as an MC is to make a 'demo CD' as an example of your work. CDs are easy and cheap to copy as gifts for friends or even to use as 'business cards' to get a gig!

After you manage to record yourself rapping, study the playback and always ask yourself four questions:

1. Can you hear your voice clearly?
2. Can you understand what you're saying?
3. Are you staying in time with the music?
4. Does it sound and feel natural?

Always listen to it as many times as you can possibly bear before making another recording. Try to write down at least three things that you'd want to improve before next time. Listen carefully to what you say and how you say it. Be patient, but also critical (after all you want to be the very best MC you can!).

YOUR GOALS

GOAL 1
To learn how to record yourself.

GOAL 2
To know how to use recordings to improve your performance.

PROBLEM?

If you find that you need to hear yourself more clearly while you're recording – but you don't want to change the balance on the recording – try taking one side of the headphones off so that you only hear the music in one ear.

IN PRACTICE

When you've practised a rhyme plenty of times and feel ready to record your voice, make sure that the recording equipment is set up properly: the microphone is plugged in (see Lesson 2), the tape is set at the beginning and the recording level is set.

STEP 1

Recording level is crucial because this establishes how much sound is going onto the tape or CD – it's a visual way of gauging sound. The recording level meter can either be a needle that swings to the right as sound is produced or, more commonly, a row of LED lights that light up as you speak and dance to the music. The trick to getting the recording levels correct is NOT to let the needle or the LED's go into the red. Keep the recording level fader or knob as high as possible, so as to get a clean and noise-free recording, but turn it down if the meters go 'into the red' more than a little bit every now and then.

Green is good
When recording a rhyme
Going to red
Is an audio crime

STEP 2

If the readings on the meters do go into the red, don't freak out – it just means that there might be some distortion on the recording. If you find the meters have gone red during a 'take' that was especially good, then be sure to check it back – you might find that it didn't distort after all (or you might even like the distortion effect!).

STEP 3

It's also worth remembering that the recording levels will change if you move the sound source (ie your mouth) further away or closer to the microphone. Experiment!

STEP 4

Remember that you'll have to use headphones when you record so that the music doesn't 'spill' into the mic and ruin the balance between the music and the rap. Some people find performing with headphones a bit awkward at first, so be sure to warm-up while wearing them.

STEP 5

The best way to connect your set-up to a recording machine is simply to connect the master outputs of a mixer (or the 'tape out' of a hi-fi) into the 'record inputs' of the recording machine. The most common machines used to make an MC recording are:

1. Cassette machine This is the easiest option and blank cassettes are cheap.

2. Reel-to-reel tape machine This is quite rare, as few people have these machines, but if you can find one, the sound is usually brilliant.

3. CDR (CD recording machine) Recordable CD machines are pretty easy and cheap to find. Blank CDs are cheap but you'll have to burn a new one for each 'take' you perform, unless you buy rewriteable CDs (on which you can record over and over).

4. Computer A computer with a decent recording and editing program is the best possible option, because it can usually record with quite good quality and, best of all, you can edit together the best bits from several takes to create one 'perfect' performance.

STEP 6

Whatever method and machine you choose, remember the most important thing is that, even if the quality is awful and the level is too loud or too soft, a good performance will always shine through.

The three important things that your demo CD should include are:

1. Good rhymes and good rapping (most important!).

2. Well-recorded material that plays back on any machine.

3. Your name on the cover (as well as a picture, if possible) and don't forget your contact details if you're looking for an audience!

EXERCISE

1. Borrow a recording machine – even if you can get one for just one day – and try recording yourself.

2. Experiment with mic distance, recording levels and maybe even a bit of distortion effect by cranking the levels just too high (some MCs use this effect all the time).

3. Listen back to your recording and analyse your performance. Think about everything from the rhymes to the recording quality. What can you improve on for next time?

TROUBLESHOOTING

One of the best things about being an MC, apart from being the life of the party, being creative and writing cool rhymes, is that the only electrical device you'll ever need is a microphone. Unfortunately, however, even the microphone can go wrong sometimes. For this last lesson, let's look at ways of solving technical problems you may come across as an MC.

YOUR GOALS

GOAL 1
To sort out distortion.

GOAL 2
To sort out feedback.

GOAL 3
To know how to fix basic mic faults.

THEORY

Distortion on a live mic is annoying because it makes the sound muffled and crackly, and it means no one can understand what you're saying. Feedback is one of the most obnoxious sounds on earth and a broken mic is more frustrating than a broken record. But you don't need to be a technical wizard to sort out these sorts of problems that MCs encounter all the time.

Let's learn how to fix
So we can throw down in the mix

IN PRACTICE

DISTORTION

STEP 1

YOUR MOUTH IS TOO CLOSE TO THE MICROPHONE! Holding the microphone too close to your mouth will result in too much air rushing into the microphone. The disc inside the microphone that reads the vibrations of your voice will be overcome with the amount of air hitting it and will not be able to give a true representation of your voice. Try moving the microphone back a little from your mouth. Also, make sure that you're not shouting into the microphone as this too can result in too much air. Practise MCing and moving the microphone into different positions around your mouth until you get the best possible sound.

STEP 2

THE MICROPHONE INPUT LEVEL IS SET TOO HIGH! Another common cause of distortion is to have the microphone input level set too high. Every mixer and hi-fi is slightly different, but most devices that accept a microphone will usually have a fader, dial or knob to enable you to adjust the amount of level or volume going into the machine. Some machines have an automatic level adjustment built in and therefore adjust automatically for the best possible sound. Always begin adjusting from the lowest position, turning it up little by little until you can hear your voice clearly.

STEP 3

THE AMPLIFIER VOLUME IS SET TOO HIGH! Some systems have an amplifier built into them and others have a separate amplifier. If the input or output volume of the amplifier is set too high then distortion may occur. Take your time setting the controls from the bottom up to minimise the amount of distortion. Always be careful not to set the volume too high as high levels of volume can damage your speakers (and your ears!).

Feedback sounds like a scream from outer space. It screeches and causes people who are nearby to run for cover. Feedback is caused when an audio 'loop' is created between the microphone and the speaker – the sound comes out of the speaker and goes right back into the mic. The amplifier keeps boosting the sound and so the screech can end up getting louder and louder unless you move the microphone away from the speakers.

STEP 1

The best way to avoid feedback is to keep the microphone well away from the speakers at all times.

MICROPHONE REPAIRS

Microphones should be sturdy since they are meant to be handled (roughly, sometimes) by the MC. Unfortunately few are sturdy enough and, of course, they tend to stop working just when you need them most. The most common fault is an intermittent 'cutting in and out' which is usually the fault of the cable rather than the mic. It occurs most often when the cable gets moved around so much during use that the tiny wires inside the cable fray or break. As the cable moves about, the wire touches and then breaks apart again causing the audio to cut in and out.

STEP 1

If you have a good quality microphone you should be able to unplug the cable from the base of the microphone for quick replacement of the cable – this is the quickest way to remedy the problem. If your mic does allow you to unplug the entire cable then the best bet is to always have a spare cable ready and waiting to plug in.

STEP 2

Repairing broken cables is much easier than most people think and can save you a fortune in new cables. All it requires is a soldering iron, some solder and a pair of wire strippers. If you decide to use a soldering iron – a cheap and reasonably easy tool to use – always read the manual and be very, very careful (they get hot!). Remember, always ask your parents' permission first!

WARNING

Remember never to touch bare electrical cables and always ask an adult to help where electricity is involved. Electrical equipment by its nature tends to require lots of external cables for speakers and amplifiers, decks and mixers, power, and so on. Always take care around the cables and try to keep them as neat as possible. Never let them lay across a floor where you may trip over them and always take extra care not to interfere with mains electricity.

MICROPHONE HUMMING

Microphones have an awful habit of picking up unwanted electrical signals from nearby power cables or appliances and this can cause a lo-pitched 'hum' to be heard in the sound system.

STEP 1

If this happens, try moving the mic cable and then try turning off each nearby device one by one until the hum disappears.

> **TIP**
>
> Take good care of your microphone. Never let it get wet (and try to keep the spit that goes into it to a minimum). Never drop it on the floor and never bend or stretch the cable unnecessarily.

EXERCISE

1. Try plugging in your mic and experimenting with different combinations of levels. Try a low level set on the mic with a high level on the mixer or the amp, then try the opposite. Notice that different combinations, even when they result in the same volume, have different qualities of sound.

TEST

QUESTION 1
Where are two places that levels can be set?

QUESTION 2
What are two causes of live distortion?

QUESTION 3
What tool can be used to repair a mic?

TOP 10 ARTISTS

MISSY ELLIOTT

EXAMPLE LYRIC

'My best friend say/ I can stay with her/ At her house no doubt/ Any time I like/ My best friend say/ Don't let you ruin my life/ Cuz you don't do for me/ And you don't act right'

TRUE STORY

When Missy was younger she used to sing to her dolls! Missy first performed as part of a neighbourhood singing group, Sista, and was lucky enough to be spotted by Jodeci.

SUPERSTAR TIP

'Stop listening to the radio for a long while before doing, playing or recording, so that you can clear your head.'

STATISTICS

DATE OF BIRTH
'That's not a question you ask a lady'

PLACE OF BIRTH
Portsmouth, Virginia, USA

INFLUENCES
Old skool, hip hop

IMPORTANT GIG/VENUE
Performing with Timbaland

BIG MOMENT
In 1991, Missy and her crew got themselves backstage passes and managed to sing to Jodeci, who signed her on the spot

PREFERRED MICROPHONE
Radio mic

IN THE STYLE OF...

Missy 'Misdemeanour' Elliott's addictive and nervy rap style often uses an almost 'stream of consciousness' feel. Her words are so natural and the flow is so relaxed that it always feels like she's making it all up on the spot. Her raw and rough language can often be 'colourful' – she is famous for telling things like she sees them and not leaving anything to the imagination. She was one of the first female MCs to be recognised as having mic skills just as good as any other rapper in history.

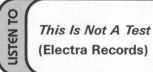

LISTEN TO

This Is Not A Test
(Electra Records)

50 CENT

EXAMPLE LYRIC

'When I apply pressure/ Son it ain't even funny/ I'm about to stick Bobby/ For some of that Whitney money'

SUPERSTAR TIP

'When I got my record deal, I would ask questions, find out what people's jobs were. If you put me in a hands-on situation, I'm gonna learn real fast. They didn't realise the importance of the black market and mix-tapes, so I used the connections I made, and did what they weren't doing.'

STATISTICS

DATE OF BIRTH
1978

PLACE OF BIRTH
Queens, NY, USA

INFLUENCES
Dr Dre

IMPORTANT BREAK
Hooking up with Jam Master Jay

BIG MOMENT
Signing to the 'Eminem Dream Team'

PREFERRED MICROPHONE
'Anything I can hold'

TRUE STORY

50 Cent's real name is Curtis Jackson. Born into a notorious Queens drug dynasty, 'Fitty' signed to Columbia Records in 1999, and was sent into a New York studio for two and a half weeks during which (relatively) short time, he made 36 tracks.

IN THE STYLE OF...

Fitty's style is an infectious, rugged flow coupled with a vicious sense of humour. As a boy, he experienced a fair amount of tough experiences and it seems to have taught him what 'drama' is all about. He spits out his rhymes fast and furious, and he lets you know he's smart but curious. Fitty often uses his own strange accent and pronunciation, but he also uses loads of '50 cent' (that is, long, unusual and difficult) words. His lyrics are eloquent, topical and heartfelt.

Get Rich Or Die Tryin'
(Interscope Records)

LISTEN TO

DYNAMITE

EXAMPLE LYRIC

'No illnesses that cannot be cured/ Better still no kind of sickness/ Everybody's got the strength of a sword/ No shots fired/ No metal detectors required/ Jealousy and greed was gone/ Paranoia expired/ All races acknowledge common likeness in all/ Finally the people stood together/ Not a chance they could fall'

TRUE STORY

Dynamite's real name is Dominic Smith. In the beginning, Dynamite wanted to be a DJ but couldn't afford the turntables. A friend got some decks and Dynamite would go round to his house to play on them, but his friend kept handing him the microphone!

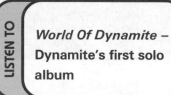

LISTEN TO

***World Of Dynamite –
Dynamite's first solo
album***

STATISTICS

DATE OF BIRTH
7 October 1973

PLACE OF BIRTH
Minden, UK

INFLUENCES
'Too many, just so many'

IMPORTANT GIG/VENUE
'No specific night – for me it was just organic'

BIG MOMENT
'When I met Roni Size and MCed with him, he liked what I did and we went to Germany and MCed there'

PREFERRED MICROPHONE
Shure SM58

IN THE STYLE OF...

Dynamite MC uses a free style that makes his raps feel fluid and spontaneous. The rapping is mostly up-tempo and fast, but still clear. His style has been compared to garage, but really it's more of a hip hop kind of MCing. He tends to start off a rap chilled out to get the listener hooked, then hypes up towards a wild finish. He uses sublime lyrics and dips in and out of the music with untouchable precision.

SUPERSTAR TIP

'I never wanted to be number one or make loads of money, so I would never be disappointed if I never made it to the top, but here I am loving every day of it.'

EMINEM

EXAMPLE LYRIC

'Stop the tape!/ This kid needs to be locked away!/ Dr Dre, don't just stand there, OPERATE!'

SUPERSTAR TIP

'Always say what you mean – it's like, I'm not alone in feeling the way I feel, I believe that a lot of people can relate to my **** – whether white, black, it doesn't matter. Everybody has been through some ****, whether it's drastic or not so drastic. Everybody gets to the point of 'I don't give a ****.'

STATISTICS

DATE OF BIRTH
17 October 1972

PLACE OF BIRTH
Kansas City, Missouri, USA

INFLUENCES
Underground hip hop

IMPORTANT GIG /VENUE
Battling schoolmates in the lunchroom

BIG MOMENT
Working with Dr Dre

PREFERRED MICROPHONE
SM58

TRUE STORY

Eminem's real name is Marshall Mathers III. After hearing Eminem freestyling on a Los Angeles radio station one day, Dr Dre tracked him down and signed him to his Aftermath label (and the rest is history).

IN THE STYLE OF...

Eminem is a lyrical gymnast who holds nothing back in his words. He can sometimes be dirty and vulgar, though he can just as often be sweet and sentimental. His records feature a technical effect on his voice called 'doubling' – achieved by recording two takes together (making it seem as if two people were rapping together). Eminem's aggressive delivery helps him create an aggressive attitude, but he cleverly undercuts this with personal and confessional lyrics. He manages to make listeners feel that they're getting 'the real person' from every rap.

LISTEN TO

8 Mile Soundtrack, *Eminem Show*, *Marshall Mathers* LP, *Slim Shady* LP (Interscope Records)

TALI

EXAMPLE LYRIC

'I'm kept awake by me/ Thinking of lyrics constantly/ I'm listening to my favourite tune/ Rehearsing versing round the room'

TRUE STORY

Roni Size was performing in New Zealand when Tali plucked up the courage to approach him and give him a blast of her MC skills. Roni was so impressed that he let Tali go on live, and it was the beginning of a beautiful relationship…

STATISTICS

STAR SIGN
Sagittarius

PLACE OF BIRTH
New Zealand

INFLUENCES
MC Dynamite, Missy Elliott

IMPORTANT GIG/VENUE
Tali had her own radio show in New Zealand and was also organising live drum'n'bass events

BIG BREAK
'Working with Roni Size in Bristol – he told me to move to Bristol and sign with Full Cycle'

PREFERRED MICROPHONE
'Any microphone that works but preferably cordless'

IN THE STYLE OF...

Tali has a very lyrical style, a soulful combination of quick-time rhymes and singing. As a trained singer and pianist, she has an instinctive knack for enhancing tunes with words. Her music is mostly drum'n'bass, and she uses a unique blend of melody and rhyme.

SUPERSTAR TIP

'Go with the flow.'

LISTEN TO

Lyric On My Lip (Full Cycle Records)

VERBALICIOUS

EXAMPLE LYRIC

'Spitting rhymes like/
Shrapnel to enemy lines/
Apocalypse from my lips/
Say your last goodbyes'

SUPERSTAR TIP

'If you're really good, your talent will shine however whack you is.'

TRUE STORY

When Verbalicious wasn't at school in the UK, she was schooling in Jacksonville, Florida, where her cousins taught her all about break-dancing and hip hop. When she returned, she found that she loved the UK scene, so started writing rhymes. One day V just took the mic at a gig and started spitting. She then started going to battles and going to open mic nights, and then Radio One turned up in her home town and she won their competition!

STATISTICS

DATE OF BIRTH
15 August 1986

PLACE OF BIRTH
Yorkshire

INFLUENCES
Old skool, soul

IMPORTANT GIG/VENUE
Radio One in 2004

BIG BREAK
Winning the Radio One competition

PREFERRED MICROPHONE
Wa'eva

IN THE STYLE OF...

Verbalicious gets right into the flow of a track and flaunts a unique blend of quick-witted lyrics. She engages her audience with a run of deep and challenging spits that are delivered with flair and style. When she feels the time is right on the night, she can up the gear with power and agility, though she always delivers a fantastic flow of rhyme that gives any tune an extra groove.

MCD

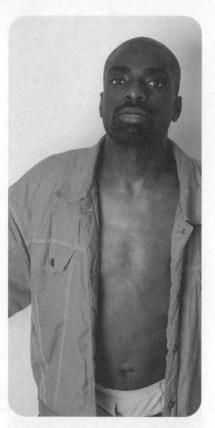

EXAMPLE LYRIC

'Looking back through life and seeing what's accrued/ All the promises we've heard and all the sugar coated words/ Travels have lead me through spiritual realms/ Where I see reasons for some things and recognise why people do dumb things/ The balance of the physical world in relation to what's needed/ Humans couldn't look at the earth and say look what we did'

TRUE STORY

MCD was once in a heavy metal band.

SUPERSTAR TIP

'If it feels good…'

STATISTICS

STAR SIGN
Taurus

PLACE OF BIRTH
London

INFLUENCES
Jay-Z

IMPORTANT GIG/VENUE
Featured rapper on the Soul2Soul remix of the Destiny's Child single 'No No No'

BIG BREAK
Supporting A Tribe Called Quest at a gig in France

PREFERRED MICROPHONE
In the studio: AKG C4000, and Live: Shure SM58

IN THE STYLE OF...

Sometimes you just want a full-tilt MC that will fire lyrics like bullets right at you – and this is the man that can deliver that recipe. MCD keeps the lyrics locked super-tight to the tune and reads the DJ perfectly to work out what will happen next.

LISTEN TO

'A wide variety of music from reggae to jazz and even classical music. Give yourself a good understanding of all music because hip hop incorporates such a wide range of influences.'

COOLIO

EXAMPLE LYRIC

'I'd be a fool to surrender when I know I can be a contender/ And if everybody's a contender then everybody could be a winner/ No matter you rag collar deep down/ We all brothers/ And regardless of the time/ Somebody else still love'

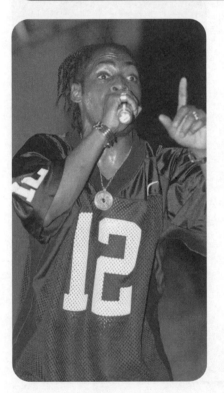

STATISTICS

DATE OF BIRTH
1 August 1963

PLACE OF BIRTH
Compton, Los Angeles, California, USA

INFLUENCES
Old skool, hip hop

IMPORTANT GIG/VENUE
Grammy Awards, as televised

BIG BREAK
Winning a Grammy Award!

PREFERRED MICROPHONE
Radio mic

TRUE STORY

Coolio was a late starter in his career, but that reminds us all that it is never too late to make it! Most rappers are already in their early 20s when they got a break; Coolio was already pushing 30 by the time his career finally took off.

SUPERSTAR TIP

'Be true to your roots, your family and yourself, always.'

IN THE STYLE OF...

Coolio's style is 'big bouncy and full of lovin', and that's why he is listened to by people all around the world. Coolio mixes hip hop-friendly party grooves with thoughtful lyrics that observe real ghetto life. He makes his lyrics roll out like silk – they grab you from the start and don't let go until the very last word, challenging everything along the way. There are no random words thrown in here or there – just pure gold and platinum rhymes.

LISTEN TO

'Gangsta's Paradise' and 'C U When You Get There' (Tommy Boy Records)

2 ICE

EXAMPLE LYRIC

'It's underground London/ Tuns of guns murders on the run/ Its bound the friction/ The poor screaming "Give me peace God"/ Why's this life so hard/ Poor people draw dole cheques/ Murders draw card/ I swear to God they're begging God/ My peoples begging God/ Why's this life so hard for me and my peeps eh yowl/ What's on these London streets'

TRUE STORY
2 Ice once recorded a single with a heavy metal band.

STATISTICS

DATE OF BIRTH
Unknown

PLACE OF BIRTH
London

INFLUENCES
Public Enemy, KRS 1

IMPORTANT GIG/VENUE
'Performing in Greece in an outdoor venue that is carved in the side of the mountains'

BIG BREAK
'When I hooded up with MCD'

PREFERRED MICROPHONE
Wa'eva

IN THE STYLE OF...

Clear your mind of old thoughts before you open your ears to 2 Ice. He describes himself as 'cold', and that's about as close to the truth as you can get. Ice's style combines dangerous lyrics performed with energy and venom, yet all put together in such a way that you still bounce around at the gig with a smile on your face. Words roll from his mouth at whatever pace is required to compliment the tune.

LISTEN TO

Dead Prez' *Let's get Free*

SUPERSTAR TIP
'I know it's hard – you gotta do it anyway'

ROOTS MANUVA

EXAMPLE LYRIC

'Overblown in the zone/ Come check the poem/ Natural things no one has shown him'

STATISTICS

DATE OF BIRTH
1974

PLACE OF BIRTH
London

INFLUENCES
Radiohead, among others

IMPORTANT GIG/VENUE
His dad is a minister in a Pentecostal church, so it was always in him to be vocal

BIG BREAK
Playing The Forum in Kentish Town, London

PREFERRED MICROPHONE
SM58

SUPERSTAR TIP

'Instead of saying you love your loved one with your vocal chords, reach deep down in yourself and speak with that inner voice…and watch the impact…It's so easy to get cynical in these big, bad corporate times – sometimes you gotta make a declaration of good hearted ghetto hoorah joyous intent.'

TRUE STORY

Roots once did a video where he pretended to go back to his old primary school to hold a sports day – but the truth is he never actually went to that school

LISTEN TO

Rakim or KRS 1

IN THE STYLE OF...

Roots is a man who can say what he thinks, yet somehow knows that his audience is thinking the same thing too. He is totally in tune with the crowd and that is a key reason why he has risen to the top of his game. He can make MCing look like a game of chess as he moves words around like pieces on the board with devastating effect. One minute he is taking you on a lyrical trip that is almost a map of your own life and thought, and then, suddenly (just as you're getting comfortable), he brings a surreal flavour into the fold. BAM, you are in a different world – the world of Roots Manuva.

CD CONTENTS

1. PAUL SEALY
'COCKTAIL BOMB'

With a big funky guitar, this track forces the MC to bounce her lyrics along with the tune. Try nodding your head along to this beat, and throw a few lyrics of your own over the top. Keep your body moving to the naturally funky pace of this tune.

2. JULIO H
'FOR THE HOODIES'

A much slower beat per minute (bpm) with big scratch samples at the start. Hold out your hand and, with a chopping motion, chop along to the drum and the MC. When you spit your own rhymes use the chopping motion to help keep your words in time.

3. ENVUS
'ALL BY CHANCE'

Listen to how the track takes a few beats to get going, and to how the MC spits his rhymes much slower, as almost like spoken word. If you're having problems dropping your rhymes, work with some slower beats to start – and don't feel you should spit lyrics over every part of the track.

4. 3 LOVE
'NOT A THING'

A much bigger, fatter track with two MCs working together to spit lyrics. Spitting lyrics with another MC takes practise as you have to take extra care not to fall over the top of each other (two lyrics at once is messy and confusing!). Listen to how they work together to avoid MCing at the same time. (They do this by listening to what the other MC is doing at all times.)

5. PAUL SEALY
'OBSERVER'

In this track the MC spits rhymes at a slow but even pace. The MC is much louder than the music, and that means he can be heard more clearly. Listen to how the MC uses a wide vocal range to express what he wants to say – he's almost singing. All the time the MC is listening to the drums to gauge the speed that he spits rhymes.

6. SLY PEEPS
'GOLD'

Listen to the conversation at the start of the track: it helps establish the MCs. The bpm of the track is much quicker, and both MCs work closely together, dropping rhymes as one at times. Also, singing parts are dropped over the track, making the track feel fuller. Try following the constant drum beat with a hand chopping movement. Listen closely to the music on the track at all times, and then listen again to the timing of the MC on the track. This will help you understand the relationship between the MC who is spitting on the track and the drums. Timing of spitting rhymes is very important.

7. PAUL SEALY
'RAP SHEET'

Now we have a full MC crew working together. Listen to how they give each other a good chance to drop rhymes. With so many of them working together they can ensure the whole track is kept busy. A space has been left at the end so you can practise spitting over the track.

8. MR BEN
'EFANES' (INSTRUMENTAL)

This track has an Eastern Promise about it. Use the beginning to spit a few words, for example spit your MC name. Once the drums start you can begin dropping your lyrics. Allow some space in your lyrical flow to give the piano sound some space to be heard. Rock your body nice and steady to the flow of the music as you drop your own rhymes over the track. You can start by spitting rhymes really slowly on this one and then speed up as you get more confident.

9. PLO
'BRAINBANK' (INSTRUMENTAL)

A really laid back track with a soft instrumental feel; but don't let that fool you, as the drum is tough. Half way through the track the MCs use some echo effect on their voices to bring a different audio dimension to the track. This track is a great example of how to hold it down nice and slowly and not race through all your lyrics.

10. DJ LIVE LEE
'BAD INTENTIONS'
(INSTRUMENTAL)

Now, with this track *you* drop slow-paced, easy, laid-back lyrics. The scratching will fill in the gaps to give you time to breathe and get your next lot of rhymes ready to spit. Use the lyrics below to get started with this track.

I spend all day at home
Rest easy 10 o'clock come
And 10 o'clock go
Play a game on the PS2
But it crash on me
I don't know what to do

Rest easy at home
11 o'clock come
And 11 o'clock go
Fix up some eats
Beans on toast no meat
Day time TV and sleep

I spend all day at home
12 o'clock come
And 12'o clock go
Maybe I'll watch TV
Just me and me
See what I can see

Now try adding some more of your own lyrics to the track.

NOTES

NOTES

NOTES

NOTES

GLOSSARY

AMP
A power-adding device that hugely increases the volume of sound that is fed into it.

AUX ('AUXILIARY')
An input on a DJ mixer or a hi-fi that allows you to connect an extra device such as a CD player or, in the absence of a dedicated mic input, a microphone.

BPM (BEATS PER MINUTE)
The speed of a song measured by how many beats are played in the space of one minute.

CANS
Another word for headphones.

DECKS (OR 'TURNTABLES')
Devices on which vinyl records are played.

DISTORTION
A crackly or broken-up sound, when the audio is not clear, usually caused by malfunction or incorrect use of a microphone.

DOUBLE SPEED
The art of MCing at twice the normal speed.

EDIT
The art of removing part of a lyric or a tune.

FADER
A volume control on a hi-fi or DJ mixer.

FEEDBACK
The loud and obnoxious whine heard when an audio 'loop' is created between the microphone and the speaker.

INTRO ('INTRODUCTION')
The beginning or 'front' of a rhyme, track or song.

LEVELS
The measure or the amount of sound that is going into a device such as a hi-fi, DJ mixer or amplifier.

MANAGER
The person who gets you gigs and makes sure you get paid.

MINI JACK
A type of small audio plug (⅛ inch) often found on portable equipment.

MINIDISC PLAYER
A portable recorder for audio.

MIXER
The box between the turntable and the hi-fi (or amp) that is used to adjust the volumes of decks (and microphones!) while mixing tracks.

PA
Public Address system. An amplified set-up, with large speakers, that is capable of generating a very loud sound.

PHANTOM POWER
A way of powering directly from the source (for special, expensive microphones) instead of plugging them into the wall.

POPPING
The sound you get if too much air rushes into the microphone, which commonly comes from saying the letter 'P' too directly into the mic.

POWERED MIC
A microphone that is powered by a battery (or by Phantom Power).

QUARTER-INCH JACK
A type of audio plug used to connect a microphone lead to a mixer (1/4 inch wide).

RADIO MIC
A microphone that doesn't have a cable attached, especially useful onstage (as you can leap around without fear of tripping over the lead).

REWIND
A silly word, often shouted by the MC or the crowd when they want to hear a record again.

RIDER
The list of things that a well-known MC will insist on having backstage, prior to playing a gig (example: five cans of coke and ten packets of salt and vinegar crisps).

SLIP MAT

The special mat that sits between the turntable platter and the record, and allows the DJ to manipulate records freely.

SM58

Industry-standard microphone, made by Shure, used by many, many MCs.

SPITTING

Dropping rhymes or doing your MC vocal thing.

TEMPO

Refers to the speed of a song.

VOCAL BOOTH

A small acoustic room used to record spitting.

WATTS

A measurement of power for audio (ie 3 watts is not very loud, while 800 watts is mighty loud).

XLR

A type of audio connector, using three pins that fit into three holes, often found on the end of the more expensive and better-quality microphone leads.

ANSWERS TO TEST QUESTIONS

LESSON 1 – MICROPHONES
1. Directional and omni-directional.
2. A cordless mic that uses a transmitter and receiver to send the sound from the mic to the desk.
3. The pickup vibrating too much.

LESSON 2 – MIC TECHNIQUE
1. The explosion sound in a mic that comes from the letter 'P', and sometimes 'D' or 'B'.
2. Use a pop shield (or 'wind cover') on the mic at all times – and carry a few spare ones to replace it when it gets wet with spit!
3. It depends on the MC, his style and whether he's rapping loudly or softly at the time.

LESSON 3 – CONNECTING UP
1. Hi-fi systems, DJ mixers and computers.
2. A feature that turns the music down automatically when the mic is on – TURN THIS FEATURE OFF.
3. Turn the mic away from the speakers.

LESSON 4 – MCING WITH A DJ
1. He keeps the music going without any stops to keep an audience dancing.
2. An EQ, or an 'equaliser', is just a fancy word for a tone control effect.
3. Echo, reverb and flanger.

LESSON 5 – WRITING RHYMES
1. Say aloud all the words you can think of that rhyme with the first word, working through the alphabet.
2. When you can't think of anything to write (but don't worry, it happens to everyone).
3. Dictionary, thesaurus (even a newspaper!).

LESSON 6 – DELIVERY
1. His style of delivery that gives him a unique identity.
2. Read them aloud – slowly and then quickly.
3. Not more than ten minutes.

LESSON 7 – MUSIC BASICS
1. To be certain of the rhythm and never lose the beat.
2. Beats per minute (bpm).
3. A tune with no singing, just music.

LESSON 8 – PERFORMING LIVE
1. The dress rehearsal before a performance, in which you make sure that everything is working properly.
2. Try breathing slowly in through your nose and out through your mouth.
3. Having fun and entertaining friends – if it ain't enjoyable, don't do it.

LESSON 9 – RECORDING
1. The tape recording becomes distorted.
2. Cassette, CDR and computer.
3. The distance between your mouth and the mic.

LESSON 10 – TROUBLESHOOTING
1. On the mixer and on the amp (and maybe even on the mic itself!).
2. Mouth too close to the mic, or level set too high.
3. A soldering iron. (But remember, ALWAYS ask your folks' permission.)